MW01244434

The Shoe Diet

The Shoe Diet

Isabelle R Shaw, PhD

Elbasy Press

The Shoe Diet
Copyright © 2007 Isabelle Raymond Shaw, PhD
Published by Elbasy Press

For further information, please contact:

www.theshoediet.com
        or
e-mail at *lesoulier@sbcglobal.net*

Photos by Susan Jackson

Book design by:

Arbor Books, Inc.
19 Spear Road, Suite 202
Ramsey, NJ 07446
www.arborbooks.com

Printed in Canada

The Shoe Diet
Isabelle R. Shaw, PhD

1. Title 2. Author 3. Self Help

Library of Congress Control Number: 2006906626

ISBN 13: 978-0-9787972-0-1
ISBN 10: 0-9787972-0-5

I dedicate this book to my wonderful husband, Paul, who on our wedding day, actually vowed to support my shoe habit for as long as we both shall live.

Table of Contents

Chapter 3

Chapter 4

Chapter 5

Chapter 6

The Shoe Diet

Preface

Not diamonds but heels are a girl's best friend.

—William Rossi

I love shoes. Wearing pretty shoes or just looking at shoes makes me happy. When I was a student, my professors would often kid around and say that I started graduate school with 40 pairs of shoes and ended up five years later with 90. If only they'd been joking…

It's true, I confess, I have a shoe problem. But I believe this to be the best problem I've ever had, and here's why: First, shoes allowed me to quit smoking. Then, shoes helped me lose weight after I quit smoking. For these two reasons, I will forever be grateful and will respect the power of shoes.

But why *shoes*? Really, do you even have to ask? If you've picked up this book, you probably know the power that shoes can have. You know how it feels when you see the perfect little heel, pump, boot, sandal, sling-back—they're all so fabulous!—and you just can't wait to try them on. Be honest, how many evenings have you spent in your pajamas walking around your house in your newest pair of shoes? And that's okay; most of us have done it. It's nothing to be embarrassed about. In fact, this will only be to your advantage and help you during your weight loss process.

Shoes actually empower you. Heels elevate you so you can see the world from a different perspective. They make you feel sexy; they make you walk a little straighter and hold your head a little higher. Shoes make you capable of anything.

Although deep down you've always known the power of shoes, you may not have quite grasped their true potential. And more importantly, you may not have been aware of their power to make you achieve *your* true potential.

This book explains the science behind the power of shoes and describes how they will help you lose weight. This is the diet you have been waiting for. This is the Shoe Diet.

Chapter 1

The Science Behind the Shoegasm

A pair of new shoes might not cure a broken heart or soothe a tension headache, but they will relieve symptoms and chase away the blues.

—Holly Brubach

S hoes have always been the cure for my blues. As far back as I can remember, looking at, trying on, or walking in beautiful shoes has always made me feel good.

No wait, I take that back. Shoes actually turn me on! Any time I have a difficult task ahead of me, I always reward myself with shoes once it's successfully finished. The thought of a beautiful pair of Manolo Blahnik black patent leather boots or Chloe silver strappy sandals really keeps me going through a week's trying moments and makes all my efforts worthwhile.

More importantly, shoes were my salvation when I was trying to lose weight. How is that possible? Well, you don't have to be a scientist to figure it out. As I am sure every woman in the world has suspected all along, shoes have the ability to stimulate the pleasure centers of the brain. After doing a little research on the subject, it turns out that these pleasure centers are anatomically connected to very important parts of our biology known as the *Reward and Motivation Systems*. These systems are critical in helping us make everyday decisions. Not only are shoes able to turn on these innate pleasure centers and reward mechanisms, they also have the ability to activate areas in the brain responsible for our emotions, motivation, memory and attention. You see, shoes actually do have the ability to control how we feel and give us the strength to accomplish pretty much anything we put our minds to.

What is even more intriguing is that by activating specific areas of the brain, pretty shoes—oh yeah, because they *do* have to be pretty—is a source of pleasure and joy that allows for the elimination of stress. In other words, the ultra-pleasant activity of shopping for shoes promotes happiness and reduces stress, both of which can help to induce healthy behavioral changes, such as losing weight.

Did you know that the French word chausson means both slipper and pastry? Coincidence? I think not.

The Neurobiology of Shoes

The human brain is a highly sophisticated and

complex structure that is made up of hundreds of millions of nerve cells called neurons. These neurons are organized into separate areas of the brain and are associated with different tasks. We are born with all of our neurons, but the connections that exist between them develop over time with each one of our experiences. Basically, our genetic backgrounds determine the overall pathways by which our neurons communicate, but they are strongly influenced by our experiences. In fact, everyday events are so important for solidifying relationships between our neurons that new experiences can alter even the most deep-rooted connections. What this means is that our brains have the ability to rewire themselves—that we have the ability to reinvent ourselves.

The human brain is a wonderful thing. The neurological pathways that are involved specifically in reward and motivation behavior have evolved over time to make us feel good for doing things that are necessary for our survival—like eating food, having sex or buying a pair of hot red Bruges platform heels. In fact, these behaviors are *crucial* for our survival and are necessary to pass along to our progeny. Another way to understand the science of evolution is that we are wired to reward ourselves for good behavior. Our survival actually depends on it!

> *In light of a life challenge such as losing weight, knowing that there will be a gorgeous pair of shoes at the end will make you stronger and more successful.*

Scientists agree that pleasure and rewards are important for promoting positive attitudes and healthy decision-making. Over the years, studies have shown that reward pathways and the sensation of pleasant emotions are linked to other structures in the brain that are involved with stress relief, motivation and emotional well-being. This makes sense, doesn't it? When we are happy and content, stress disappears, and we do anything to prolong these good feelings. Much research has been conducted to show that pleasurable sensations actually cause the release of neurochemical substances known as endorphins, which have soothing, anti-stress properties and further extend the feeling of pleasure. The secretion of these neurochemical substances is crucial for the perfect shoegasm.

What is a shoegasm? Come on, you know exactly what it is: that rush and excitement you feel when you find the most amazing pair of shoes! And yes, there is actually a scientific explanation for it. The reward pathways I mentioned before are connected with other areas of the brain that work to enhance our emotional experiences. So when the brain reward systems are turned on by, let's say, a pair of Christian Louboutin leopard pumps, an emotional transformation sets in. This emotional transformation can range from mild satisfaction to highly intense bliss—in other words, a shoegasm—and therefore helps to direct us toward a natural reward, or a reward-seeking behavior. Basically, what this means is that the way our brains are structured makes it possible for us to seek rewards for our efforts, leading us, in this case, to our favorite shoe store.

I remember exactly when I started realizing the power that shoes can have. It all started with a bad hair day—you know how crazy bad hair days can make you and how they also inexplicably set the tone for the whole day. Well, aside from my hair having a mind of its own, it was also one of those days when anything and everything went wrong. To top it all off, I received an email informing me that my latest manuscript had been rejected again. I sat there in my chair, staring at the reflection of my bad ponytail in my computer screen, thinking that I should have just stayed in bed. By five o'clock, I was in desperate need of something to make me feel better. Walking home, I was thinking of all the comfort food options I could have for dinner, and just when I had decided on a big bucket of deep-fried chicken, I caught a glimpse of a really cute pair of gold wedge sandals in a shop window. So I walked in. One hour later, after trying on half the shoes in the store, I thanked the salesgirl for her time and effort—especially since I hadn't bought anything. But you know, when I walked out of the store, I couldn't even remember why I'd been so upset. I'd forgotten all about the bad day, the bad hair and the bucket of chicken.

The Memory of Shoes

Scientific studies have shown that the sensation of pleasure, rewarding behavior and memory are all biologically unified. In fact, it's been shown that even without experiencing an actual reward, just the memory of past pleasures—or virtual bliss—can be a powerful motivator.

Now this concept is especially important because it means is that the mere fact of daydreaming about those beautiful Gucci gold satin corset heels can bring on the good vibrations—a virtual shoegasm, if you will, leaving you relaxed and glowing! What you need to remember from this is that shoegasms, or just the memory of them, can reinforce healthy decisions and, for instance, make you stay on the treadmill a little longer. In fact, the association between virtual bliss and wholesome foods can actually trigger a positive bodily sensation, which results in immense reinforcement for our overall healthy behaviors.

Now here's where it all begins to make sense. How will shoes actually help you lose weight? It's pretty simple actually: The power of shoes—the emotional positive sensation that invades you when you're trying on a pair of Chanel Cambon ballerina flats—activates the reward pathways we've been discussing. So if you are used to activating your reward centers with food, beautiful silk stilettos will stimulate those same pathways and create similar physiological effects, leaving you blissful and happy with your fabulous new pair of shoes, and none of the calories.

So the only question left is this: Do you want a new pair of shoes or not?

Isabelle R Shaw, PhD

Shoegasm Centers of the Brain

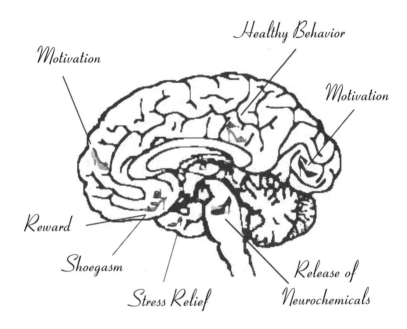

Motivation

Healthy Behavior

Motivation

Reward

Shoegasm

Stress Relief

Release of
Neurochemicals

Chapter 2

Shoe Cravings for Food Cravings

If shoes don't hurt, they don't have style.

—Erma Bombeck

hate to be the bearer of bad news, but there really is no magical way to lose weight. You gain weight when you eat more calories than you burn, and you lose it by eating fewer calories and being more active, and that's about the extent of it. The number of calories you eat (and drink!) and the number of calories you burn determine your weight. It's that simple.

However, we all know how hard that really is to put into practice. Why? because it requires that you make conscious efforts, conscious choices, and stick with them. So the bad news is that it's going to be tough to lose weight. But the good news is that there are certain things you can do that will make it easier—and they involve shoes!

First and foremost, you have to want to do it. Realizing that there is no one else who can do it for you is the first real step. This is your decision. You are the only one who decides what you put in your mouth and you are the only person who can decide to get up and exercise. Invest in yourself. You have one body, so why treat it badly when you can treat yourself to new shoes instead?

So it's all up to you. Of course, it's easier said than done, but you should know that it *can* be done. Just think about this: If you're the one who's doing all the hard work, don't you deserve a great new pair of shoes?

To this day, I still remember my first craving. It was January 2003. The temperatue outside was something ridiculous like -22 F. My best friend was visiting with her uncle from France (who, you may imagine, was not enjoying the weather). We were sitting in a little bistro, smoking and enjoying great wine, ripe cheeses and other delectables. Well, at least they were: I just sat there salivating and depressed. I couldn't concentrate on anything they were saying. It took every ounce of energy that I had to control the urge to give in and quit my diet. It really sucked.

After what seemed like hours, we decided to walk over to another restaurant for dinner (did I mention that the delectables were only the appetizers?). As I was putting on all three of my coats—it was -22 out there!——I thought that I would just go home, because I was miserable. But as we walked to the restaurant, the cravings passed. Was is the cold? Or maybe the restaurant change? Who knows? The point is, I had survived. At that moment, I was so proud of myself that I decided that I so deserved those cute shoes I'd seen online the week before. You just have to love lime green kitten heels in the dead of winter!

Your Best Foot Forward

Okay, so you know it's not going to be easy, but there are some ways to make the weight loss process more bearable.

First of all, don't try to lose weight by yourself. One of the best ways to be successful is to have friends and family who are supportive of your decision. Surround yourself with people who encourage you—and maybe even join you! A good support system can go a long way. Moreover, do not get weighed down by people who don't support your decision, who don't care or who even want to see you fail. Keep your distance from them so they don't drag you away from your goal. Of course, there are those who may not quite understand your love of shoes and think you're harebrained, and that's okay. Just don't let them shoe-shame you. As long as *you* have faith in the power of shoes, you will succeed.

Natural habits

We're all creatures of habit. We do things throughout the day without even thinking about them. We do them because over time, we have trained our bodies to do so. In fact, our bodies respond and react to our daily routines to the point that we can go through a series of complicated behaviors without even realizing it.

This is absolutely true of our eating habits. We eat when we're hungry, but we also eat as part of a routine, or just because food is in front of us. As a consequence, we have trained ourselves to have unhealthy eating patterns—a bag of chips in the car on the way back from the grocery store, a tub of ice cream when we're having a bad day. What's worse is that when doing this, you can actually trick your body in thinking you're hungry when you're in those situations, even though you're not.

But don't worry, these are habits that you can modify. The body and mind constantly react to our environment, like when you're walking toward the kitchen to make dinner and glance at the washing machine, which causes you to throw in a load of laundry. An environmental cue can trigger or change a behavior—it's a great trick that you can definitely use to your advantage. One way to do this is to put out your cute, new running shoes before you go to bed at night so that you'll see them first thing in the morning, and that alone can make you want to get out there and get your body moving.

Stressful Times

If you're used to heading for the refrigerator the second you're stressed out, here is where you may be able to make the biggest impact. With time and determination, this habit can be modified! For example, instead of reaching for the pantry door, go for a walk, meditate, sing, dance—whatever it takes. Just do not eat if you are not hungry! Do anything else but eat. It will be difficult, but remember that it's just a habit, and you have the power to change it. Working hard at this will definitely be worth the fabulous shoes coming your way.

To know yourself is to be successful, and it really does help when you can identify which tricks help you and which don't. Figure out what works for you and stick to it. You know what they say: If the shoe fits, buy it in every color.

Here's a little trick I learned to help me figure out if I'm actually hungry or just tempted by yummy looking food: I reach for an apple. If I'm really hungry, I eat it. If not, I go online to check out new Jimmy Choo listings on eBay. It totally works for me!

Isabelle R Shaw, PhD

Realistic Goals

Wouldn't you love to lose 50 pounds in four weeks? Ah, hell, wouldn't we all? But chances are, it will not happen. First, it's just not healthy and second, it's not a realistic goal. Do yourself a favor and don't set yourself up for failure.

Instead, create weekly goals for yourself that you can actually accomplish, so that you can reach them and celebrate your success. Think about it: If you had to wait months for a reward, how much would you feel like exercising every day? Probably not very much. However, if you go through every week with feelings of success, you'll be more motivated to continue on your diet. That way you'll work out and eat right consistently, and your weight won't fluctuate back and forth, making you feel like you're not achieving anything.

Whether you choose to reward yourself every day, every week, or every month is up to you. However, for the first few weeks, do try to keep your reward intervals short enough for you to keep a goal in mind and reach it. Remember, if you go too long without a reward, it might be harder to keep yourself on track, and you might lose steam.

But as time goes by, and as new habits set in, rewards can be more spaced out. Everyone is different, so do what works best for you.

By sticking to your realistic goals, healthy habits will set in and become part of your daily routine. It may take longer than you hope, but you will get there by taking small steps in your fabulous new shoes.

Chapter 3

The First Pair

It's impossible not to smile when you wear a pair of shoes.

—Andrea Pfister

T he Shoe Diet is based on the principle that any obstacle, such as losing weight, should be viewed as a challenge. Knowing that there will be a positive reward once a goal is accomplished will shape your happiness, health and well-being. One of the crucial points of the Shoe Diet is that you must allow yourself to enjoy a reward for hard work, and enjoy feeling good about yourself. The happiness that shoes produce will not only effectively reduce stress, but it will also help to promote a positive attitude and healthy decisions that will make you stronger throughout the weight loss process.

Let's face it, losing weight is not going to be easy, but it can be a very realistic ambition. And doesn't the idea of using shoes to motivate you even sound a little bit like fun? What on earth can be more motivating than an amazing pair of Giuseppe Zanotti ankle strap jewel encrusted heels?

You just never know . . .

I can remember when I first started my diet. I wanted to be healthy, so every time I went to the mall, I would have a fruit smoothie. There I was, walking along, looking for shoes to reward myself with for a week of regular elliptical training. I thought I was being good, but I later found out that my "healthy snack" was worth 500 calories. That's the same amount as a quarter-pound hamburger!

The First Step

In order to reward yourself with your first pair of shoes, you must take the first step toward good behavior: Begin a food journal. This is simply a notebook where you write down everything that you ingest for the next two weeks. That's right: *everything*. Everything you eat, everything you drink, and everything you put on what you eat or drink. This includes breakfast, lunch, dinner, snacks, lattes, candy, smoothies—*everything*. Just because you don't chew doesn't mean it doesn't count. Statistics show that you may be drinking 20 percent of your daily calorie intake. That's actually double what it should be. So write it *all* down.

That's how you start. Pretty easy, isn't it? Well, okay, there is a little more you need to do, but it's really not so bad. Here's a list of all you need to write down in your food journal:

1. The time

2. The type of food

3. The quantity and the calories

4. The location

5. Your mood

6. Was it worth it?

Most of these categories are self-explanatory, but you may be wondering about a few of them. First, let's talk about location. Remember when I was talking about how we're creatures of habit, and we do things throughout the day without even thinking about them? That's what I was doing, every time I went to the mall and had a smoothie without even thinking about it. More importantly, I didn't even question whether I was hungry or not! I just knew that I was at the mall, so it must be time for a smoothie. Writing down where you eat or drink will actually help you to realize that you may have developed some location-related habits that need to be broken.

The same idea applies to writing down your mood. Remember my bad hair day? When my first comforting thought was about food? A big bucket of fried chicken, no less. Pay attention to your mood and it will help you identify why you're eating or what mood triggers you to eat. I said it before, and I'll say it again—to know yourself is to be successful. So every time you eat or drink, write down whether you are happy, sad, stressed, tired, bored, anxious, or whatever. You may be shocked by how much your emotions can make you eat when you really don't need to.

Okay, now for the "Was it worth it?" question. It should be no surprise that sometimes you probably eat mindlessly, or eat when you're not enjoying or even tasting anything anymore. Yet, you keep on eating. For example, you're in a great restaurant and you order an enormous piece of chocolate cake for dessert. It's absolutely delicious but after several good bites, you're full and don't really want anymore, but you eat it all anyways. Or again, it could be that the cake is quite horrible tasting, but again you eat it because after all, you are paying for it. Honestly, in hindsight, was it really worth it?

So here's what you do: Anything you eat, rate how gratifying it was on a scale of one to five, using a shoe rating system. Think of it just like a hotel star system, with one shoe corresponding to "not really worth it" and five shoes meaning "it was *so* worth it!" When you rate each item, keep in mind the number of calories it contained, and based on that, decide whether it was still worth it overall. Do you think you could be as satisfied with half?

To give you an idea of how to get started, I've included an example of a food journal at the end of the book that you can fill out.

The portions served in restaurants these days are so *huge,* it's hard to recognize what a "normal" portion is anymore. You can easily make two if not three servings out of one meal from a restaurant. Don't be compelled to eat it all in one sitting just because you're paying for it. Keep the other half for dinner, or for lunch the next day. In this way, you eat less and you spend less on food, which leaves you with more money for shoes!

Isabelle R Shaw, PhD

Reality Bites

Throughout the next two weeks, as you fill in your food journal, you will start noticing certain patterns or unhealthy eating habits that you've developed over time. For example, you may realize that when you walk past the vending machine after work, you always buy a chocolate bar to eat in the car on the way home. Or, you may notice that when you go on a break with your colleagues, you always need a caramel latte. But these are eating patterns that can be modified—knowing that you even have them is the first step to making that change.

Don't get discouraged if all this seems hard at first. It would be somewhat naïve to think that you can improve your eating habits right away. You can't change overnight, and like I told you before, don't set yourself up for failure. Give yourself a chance by setting realistic goals, and rewarding yourself often.

Speaking of a realistic goal, how about starting like this? Once you identify those items with the one-shoe rating, begin cutting them out of your diet. This is a great way to start because chances are, these are items you eat just because they're there, and not because they're really "worth it." You will not miss them at all!

For the following week, maybe try cutting back on those five-shoe items you love. Eat them less often or only eat half of what you're used to. Better yet, try to find a healthier version that you actually like. When you take pleasure in the healthy foods you eat, it's definitely a lot easier to make a change.

You need to remember that the idea is not to eliminate everything that you enjoy in your diet, but to make you realize what, when and why you are eating. The food journal will also help you learn about the foods you're eating and just how many calories you're consuming every day. Of course, you want to be able to enjoy everything you eat, but you want to eat everything in moderation as well. For now, though, you should just concentrate on your current eating habits and focus on filling out your food journal. We'll talk about the concept of moderation in more detail in Chapter 5.

Each week, make a plan for yourself. Be inventive, but again, be realistic. And when you find yourself longing for a double portion of your five-shoe favorite, focus on the gorgeous heels you've had your eyes on. They will be yours at the end of the week.

Make sure your new shoes reflect your efforts for the week. Use the shoe rating system as your guide, and reward yourself accordingly. If you're working hard on cutting back on your favorite five-shoe food items, give yourself multiple shoegasms that week.

Now you have a plan, so get going, be creative and be realistic. You are well on your way to a fabulous new pair of shoes.

Chapter 4

Moving in Your Shoes

Nothing has been invented yet that will do a better job than heels at making a good pair of legs look great, or great ones look fabulous.

—Stuart Weitzman

O kay, so you know that the number of calories you ingest and the number of calories you burn will determine your weight. You know that it's all about eating less and exercising more. In the previous chapter, you learned why and how to keep a food journal. You've also learned to try to identify unhealthy eating patterns in order to make positive changes. Now comes the part about exercising more.

Use Your Shoes

What's the point of buying a new pair of shoes if you're not going to use them? And by using them, I mean walking, running, dancing, hiking, rollerblading (sure, rollerblades count as shoes, why not?), or whatever gets you on your feet and moving. The goal is to burn energy. If whatever you're doing in your shoes burns off more calories than you're consuming in your daily diet, then you're on the right track to another new pair of shoes.

I hate running. I really do. It hurts physically, and it actually hurts me mentally. The first time I went running, I was so miserable. It was over after only 10 minutes and I wanted to cry, but more than anything else, I just wanted to breathe!

Unfortunately, the second time was not much better, but I kept at it for 15 minutes—and yes, I still wanted to cry. But I kept doing it, because I was determined to do it. I had also sworn to myself that if I could run for 20 minutes straight, those black leather boots I had seen at my favorite shoe store were mine! Let me tell you, when I was running and nauseous and seeing stars, I clung to those boots for dear life.

The first day I wore the boots, it was pure happiness. Every time I wore them after that, I was reminded of how I had accomplished *something I never thought I could do, and I really felt great. Now, if that's not motivation to keep it up, I don't know what is!!*

What you should take from that little story of mine is that you can be smarter than I was: Don't begin an exercise plan with the one physical activity you hate the most. Walking is always a great first choice, but don't limit yourself. Try biking or swimming, or any other sport that suits your personal taste. Be creative, but still be realistic.

If you're one of those people who enjoys going to a gym to exercise, that's great! Be sure to use all of the services your gym offers by asking a trainer to help you develop a weekly exercise plan. If you have a hard time staying on a treadmill, try one of the full-hour classes your gym offers, or simply switch to another type of machine. Maybe you're a Stair Master in training and you didn't even know it.

For the others who just can't bear the thought of a gym, think outside the box. Be inventive. Try kickboxing or other martial arts; give fencing a try, or yoga, or Pilates or ballroom dancing. Shake your stuff in the privacy of your own living room or even while you do the dishes after dinner. Find ways to move that are fun for you, or at least not too miserable. Go out and play, and try to do it every day, or at least three to five times a week.

Qui dort, dine *

Did you know that sleep can actually help you to lose weight? Your body responds better to weight loss if you sleep close to eight hours a night. Sleeping well will also allow you to dream about how fantastic you'll look in your new shoes!

*French Proverb which means, "She who sleeps, also eats."

On the Move

There are many ways to stay active throughout the day. If you have an hour for lunch, use most of it to walk. If you have errands, do them on foot, not in the car. It's not hard to find time to move! Even just getting a friend to walk with you to your favorite shoe store to check out the latest arrivals is good.

Here's an idea: For your first pair of reward shoes, get yourself a great, cute pair of comfy flats to use as walking shoes. But please, don't ever wear white sneakers, with any work outfit, EVER! There are so many attractive and comfortable walking shoes available these days that there's no excuse for anyone to sport that look ever again! I may not be the fashion police, but I am a fashion scientist, so please trust me on this one.

If there is just no way that you can stop midday for a brisk walk, then try doing it before or after work. In addition, you can take the stairs whenever possible to get in a few extra steps. If you need to go grocery shopping after work, then walk with your groceries in your hands back to your car. Use your imagination—it all accumulates, and it's all worth it. If you go to the mall, park your car at the farthest end

Get a Pedicure

As you first begin to exercise, your feet will take a beating, so make sure you care for them on a regular basis. Get yourself some fancy foot lotions or super plush slippers. Take a break from your favorite heels and get a pedicure or a foot massage. Make this ritual part of your reward and alternate it with shoe shopping once in a while. When your feet are healthy, it will make exercising a lot easier...not to mention how pretty they will look in sandals and a cute toe ring!

of the parking lot. Walk around the entire mall at least once before you go into any shops. With the size of malls today, this may take you 30 to 40 minutes! That counts! Who knew? Shopping really is exercise.

*O*nce I realized how much I had to move in order to burn calories, making healthier eating decisions became easier. I can remember one time when I was in line at the grocery store after a session at the gym, and I caught a glimpse of the chocolate bar display. Since I had just worked out, I thought, Why not? Then I looked at the nutritional content and realized that I would have to go back to the gym after I ate one. From that point on, I looked at food items in terms of the amount of activity needed to burn them off. Think about it—there are between 140 and 200 calories in regular soft drinks. That's 25 minutes worth of walking!

If you only have 30 minutes, then try more intense exercise—within your personal limits—to burn off as many calories as possible. In the following table, you can get an idea of the number of calories that are burned with different types of exercise and chores. There are other resources like these that can be extremely helpful, so use this information to your advantage.

Activity	If you weigh 200 lbs*	If you weigh 300 lbs*
Ironing (30 min)	102 Cal	153 Cal
Walking up stairs (10 min)	122 Cal	183 Cal
Housework (1 hour)	264 Cal	396 Cal
Shopping (1 hour)	216 Cal	324 Cal
Walking 4mph (40 min)	312 Cal	468 Cal
Gardening (1 hour)	492 Cal	738 Cal
Mopping (20 min)	136 Cal	204 Cal

* Based on calculations taken from
www.healthstatus.com.

Chapter 5

They're Not Called Power Heels for Nothing

Give a girl the correct shoe and she can conquer the world.

—Bette Midler

on't you just love that quote? It's so true! Gorgeous shoes have always given me confidence. I remember my first board meeting; I was 26 years old and barely out of school. I was so very nervous, and I kept asking myself how the heck all those doctors were going to take me seriously. What had I gotten myself into? So I decided to wear my latest power shoes: a beautiful pair of black patent d'Orsay 3 ½-inch heels. And I thought to myself, if they see me walking into the boardroom wearing these heels, they will have to think, wow, if she can walk in those heels, she can do anything!

Okay, so chances are, none of those doctors noticed my shoes. But I walked into that room knowing that I *could* do anything. After all, it takes a talented woman to walk in those heels. And just so you know, the meeting went very well, and as it turned out, I was elected chairperson the following year.

This just goes to show that when you have a little faith in yourself, you really can do anything you put your mind to, including losing weight.

Anything worth doing is worth doing in a fabulous pair of shoes.

When All Else Fails, All You Need is Fabulous Shoes

There are countless diets out there, and I am sure that you are familiar with many of them. Some are complicated, some are ridiculous and some are even pointless. The truth is that the only way to effectively lose weight and keep it off is to reduce your caloric intake by eating less, and exercise more. You know this is true, even though it's not been easy to accept. We all want to take the easy route, and when there's news of a new, fast-acting diet, it's always so tempting to believe that this will be the one.

Regardless of what you have done in the past, if you have ever attempted to lose weight, you know it's not going to be easy. As a matter of fact, you know that it's going to suck. Giving up something that tastes good and that you enjoy is just not something you would want to do. Who would?

However, what you have to realize is that you don't have to give anything up completely. You should never totally deprive yourself of those five-shoe items you love—that just makes no sense at all! What you need to do is learn how to enjoy them in moderation. There are so many calories you can ingest in one day—usually around 2000, depending on your weight—and it really is up to you to decide how you're going to eat them. This will require that you re-learn how much and what to eat, and basically change your lifestyle. And that, my shoe-loving friend, is definitely going to be a challenge.

Change is a scary thing. And for some reason, we often assume that change is bad before we even know what it entails. That's actually the biggest barrier to any accomplishment, so it's crucial that you understand exactly what "lifestyle change" means in order to get over that barrier.

Don't assume right from the start that being on a diet means that you'll be chained to a treadmill and eating lettuce for the rest of your life. That's a big misconception—it's just not true! Think about change as an opportunity to learn something new. Think about how you're going to discover new foods and new healthy meals that you never knew were so good. Or, you may find a sport that you're really good at. You might even remember how much fun it is to dance. There will be some difficult times ahead, because it's not easy to break habits you've had all your life. But you must remind yourself that for every difficult and trying moment you face and successfully overcome, there will be shoes to reward your efforts. Invest in yourself. You are worth it.

All the Celebrities Are Doing It

I'm sure that right now you're thinking, *There has to be a better or easier way to lose weight!* I know it's hard to accept this, especially when so many advertisements out there promise revolutionary and easy ways to lose weight. And of course, they are always scientifically proven to work effortlessly!

Don't be fooled. You know better. The reality is that fad diets don't last. They may help you lose weight in the beginning, but what happens after a while? You gain it all back and then some. I know this may seem like I'm saying the same thing over and over, but if you want to lose weight efficiently and keep it off, you have to make a lifestyle change. There is no other way. Think about it: If there were any other way, why would the most powerful, rich and resourceful celebrities be eating less and exercising more to lose weight?

> *Give a girl a pair of shoes, and she'll feel good for a day.*
>
> *Teach her how to buy shoes and she'll look fabulous for a lifetime.*

Whether you realize it or not, you are embarking upon a lifelong challenge. This is true whether you're trying to lose 10, 50 or 100 pounds. It's worth doing well from the very beginning, which means you are going to have to do your homework. Ask yourself questions about the foods you are consuming, such as, how many calories do your favorite foods actually contain? How many portions are you really eating? Pay attention to labels, especially if you eat pre-packaged foods. Also, ask yourself how much you would have to exercise in order to balance your daily caloric intake. Take the time to learn about this stuff because it will help you to identify and reach your goals.

Did you know that it actually takes a substantial amount of calories to maintain your current weight? It turns out that halting weight gain can translate into consuming 100 fewer calories a day. This is the equivalent of leaving the last three bites of a hamburger on your plate! And did you know that drastically cutting back on food actually threatens the body? It slows down the rate at which calories are burned and makes weight loss more difficult. So it's important to make gradual changes in your eating habits. Learning little facts like these can make a huge impact on your weight loss process.

It's a lot easier to be successful when you know what you're doing and how to do it. As mentioned in Chapter 3, filling out your food journal is a great way to learn about yourself. When you realize how many calories you are ingesting out of habit, when you are not hungry, you can easily work on changing those habits and on replacing them with healthier choices.

But what about when you actually *are* hungry? And what about those four and five-shoe favorites that are *so* worth it? Don't give them up! If they are high in calories (as I'm sure they are), just eat less of them, less often. Or, learn how to make a lower-calorie version. As for other foods that are low-cal, you can eat more of them—it's that simple. You need to learn how to eat in moderation, and if you're not sure what foods to eat or what "moderation" means, that's where the homework comes in. Where can you look for this information? There are countless guides and guidelines that are published in books or online. To help you get started, I've included the addresses of several websites for you at the end of this book.

The point here is not to tell you what and how much to eat. You need to figure out what works for you and what you actually enjoy, and where you can make the most changes in your diet. You know your eating habits better than anyone else, and you know what foods you like most. You are in control of your decisions. It's just easier to make better and healthier decisions when you have the information you need.

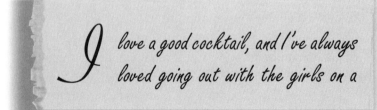

I love a good cocktail, and I've always loved going out with the girls on a

Friday night and showing off my new shoes. I always used to start the evening with a Black Russian with four cherries—that's 250 calories a pop! Who knew? Then I found out that a Mai Tai has 310, and a Singapore Sling? 230! I DIDN'T KNOW! It's not like drinks have a label on them or anything! So now when I go out, I enjoy one cocktail and then switch to a glass of wine or a vodka soda. They're around 70 calories a glass.

Your weight loss process should be a priority that you work at everyday. But you need tools. How can you be expected to know how to lose weight if you don't have the right tools? Sure, it would be great to hire a chef who could figure it out for you and a trainer to kick your butt into shape. Hey, if you can do either or both, then great! But you need to realize that you eventually have to do the work yourself. And let me tell you, if you are doing the work, you deserve the shoes!

All the information you need is out there, so take advantage of it and make the right decisions. Certain foods can be deceiving and may contain a lot more calories than you ever thought. "Low fat", "low carb" or "low protein" do not mean low in calories, so pay attention to labels and to what you are eating. Also, some salads (usually because of the dressing) have the same if not more calories than two slices of pizza! Be smart and educate yourself; this will only make you more successful.

When trying to moderate what you eat, you'll need some tricks. Learn healthier ways to prepare your favorite foods. For instance, just baking a piece of chicken instead of frying it can make a huge difference in the number of calories. Or, if you love steak, throw a four-ounce filet on the barbecue and fill the rest of your plate with grilled veggies. Replace a hamburger patty with a Portobello mushroom. It's so good!

If you prepare your meals, you can better control portions as well as calories. And, it's so much less expensive than eating out! If you don't know how to cook, there are so many resources around to help you learn. There's a whole network on television devoted to cooking, or you can get a cookbook, or

If you are used to going out for lunch every day, try bringing something from home (such as leftovers from the night before) two or three times a week instead. You still get to go out for lunch on occasion and socialize with friends, but at the same time, you save money by not going out every day. You also get to eat something that you made, which may be a lot healthier than what you will get when eating out.

even take lessons, which are available in many local grocery or cooking stores. Again, you need to be creative. Another good alternative is taking one diet plan in particular that works for you and rewarding yourself for following it.

You deserve to be the best and healthiest you can be, and more importantly, you *can* do it. Give yourself some credit and you'll realize what you can actually do. You will be amazed. What's more, you will look amazing during every step of this weight loss process in your gorgeous new shoes. What I've learned from experience is that in return, those shoes will remind you of what you have accomplished and just how amazing you really are. That's priceless.

Chapter 6

The Power of Shoes

I still have my feet on the ground, I just wear better shoes.

—Oprah Winfrey

Y ou must respect the power of shoes. Even though you will deserve every pair of shoes you earn as a reward, you do not deserve to put yourself in debt.

Sure, But I Can't Afford Manolos

Let's face it, not many of us can afford Manolo Blahniks, let alone one pair every week. The point is not to feel guilty about what you are spending, because that will just defeat the whole purpose, stress you out and, chances are, make you head straight for the fridge.

You have to follow the Shoe Diet within your budget. In this day and age, there are enough very cute and inexpensive shoes to go around. There are so many shoe stores out there that can fit any lifestyle, so you will have plenty of options to choose from. If you're on a tight budget, that's fine. Believe it or not, I did it on a yearly salary of less than $15,000. I still paid my rent, still had a life and did not go into debt.

If you think about how much money you spend on your muffin or bagel, your large café mocha with caramel and double cream (which, by the way, has more calories than one meal), your vending machine snacks and lunch out in a restaurant, you are spending a nice little sum every day. By removing these items from your daily routine you are, first of all, eliminating a significant number of calories from your diet, and second, you are also saving quite a bit of money. It all adds up! Even if you save as little as $10 a day (which otherwise pays for two specialty coffees), that's $50 a week! You can get a really cute pair of shoes for $50. As a matter of fact, you can probably get two pairs of shoes!

Tell-Tale Shoes

If you're feeling anything other than pure happiness after purchasing your shoes, then they are no longer a reward. Remember that one of the crucial points of the Shoe Diet is that a reward must be enjoyed—it must make you feel good about yourself. If you don't, this could mean that you spent too much money on them.

What you will come to realize is that it's not about how much money you spend on your shoes. You can spend three dollars on a pair of flip-flops and feel fabulous wearing them. Why? It's what they symbolize. If those flip-flops represent the triumph of losing 15 pounds, you will wear them often and proudly. Think of all your shoes as little wearable trophies, and give them names, like *My I-just-went-two-weeks-without-eating-potato-chips-and-I-lost-three-pounds shoes.* Or again, *my I-can-now-complete-30-minutes-of-cardio-non-stop shoes.*

If your shoes are not rewarding, it could also mean that you did not follow your plan and therefore don't deserve them. The thing is, if you don't deserve them, you shouldn't buy them. If for some reason you're not able to reach your goal for any given week, then no shoes for you! But don't get discouraged. Instead, just try to reach your goal the following week, or modify your goal to make sure you are successful.

Don't beat yourself up, but still, don't reward yourself for not following your diet plan. What would be the point? Actually, when you think about it, you can do anything you want, really, because there is no shoe police and no one is checking in on you to make sure that you are not cheating. But let me ask you this: Who do you think you're cheating? You are cheating yourself. Now, why would you want to do that?

I have a sensational pair of heels that I've never worn. I bought them after a week when I had made a plan to run a total of 15 miles. Maybe it was too much too fast, because I only went running once that week and ran just one mile. A far cry from my goal, but I still figured that I deserved my weekly reward for my efforts. Actually, I had seen a fantastic pair of heels and I was going to buy them regardless of what I had done that week.

When I got home, it was strange, because I didn't take them out of their box and put them on right away, as I usually do with new shoes. They stayed in their box for a week. I was excited to get to wear them the next Friday night at last, but when I put them on, they didn't look so good anymore. All I could think about was the fact that I had not run the miles I had planned to run. I had cheated and I didn't *feel good wearing them. So I put them back in their box, and back in my closet. They've been there ever since.*

If your conscience doesn't keep you grounded, then you will quickly realize that a pleasant activity will turn into an unpleasant experience. Scientific studies have actually shown that different brain areas are activated if a pleasant activity is no longer rewarding. What this means is that shoes can lose their power and actually turn off the pleasure centers and reward mechanisms of the brain. So if you are not using your shoes as a reward for your hard work, pleasure centers will not be activated, and there will be no highly intense bliss and no stress release. My friend, there will be no more shoegasms! So please, do yourself a huge favor and do not allow shoes to lose their power.

You may be wondering how many pairs of shoes it will take to get you to succeed. The answer is very simple: AS MANY AS IT TAKES! You only have one body, so aren't you worth every penny you spend on your health? You might still think that you can't afford this diet, but let me ask you this: How much do you think gastric bypass surgery costs? The average price ranges from $15,000 to $20,000. Do you know how many pairs of shoes you can get for that much money? And what nobody ever tells you is that after surgery, if you don't change your lifestyle, you will gain most of your weight back. The Shoe Diet is a lot less risky and definitely a lot more fun. And if that doesn't convince you that you are worth it, then think of all the shoes!

The Sweet Shoe of Success

*T*here was a time, after many months on the Shoe Diet, that I thought to myself how ridiculous it was to have spent all that money on shoes. After all, I was still a graduate student, making less than $15,000 a year. I went into my closet and looked closely at each pair that I had. They were all nicely arranged and looked so pretty in their places, and then I remembered when I'd purchased each and every one of them and why. The navy blue and cream spectators—that was after a whole month of going to the gym three times a week. The magenta square-toe pumps—I got those after I finished my exams without having one cigarette. The purple snakeskin boots (they're still hot!) came home with me after I had actually lost 10 pounds.

Each pair put me back through the emotions of each trying moment, when the only thing that kept me going was the thought of getting those shoes. So it had worked—I had done it and I truly deserved every single pair in my closet. I invested in my health and I succeeded. And let me tell you, there's nothing sweeter than wearing your success.

Note from the Author

o paraphrase Oscar Wilde, "If you want to tell people the truth, promise them shoes, otherwise they'll kill you." It's not easy to tell people that they need to lose weight. I know it's not pleasant to hear and trust me, it's not pleasant to say. But it does need to be said. And my way of saying it is by sharing my knowledge of the power of shoes.

But really, why shoes? Because shoes make you feel sexy regardless of what size you are. I know what it's like to go shopping for clothes and finding that nothing fits right, that everything is too small. It's just so depressing and demoralizing. But for some reason, this never seems to happen with shoes. You can always find a pair that makes you feel great. And when you feel good about yourself, you are more likely to have a positive attitude, challenge yourself and treat yourself well.

And that's why I wrote this book—because I know there are many shoe lovers out there who could benefit from it. Whether you are obese, overweight or just trying to lose 10 pounds, it really is important to bring yourself down to your personal healthy weight. If you're not sure what that weight should be, then talk to your doctor. If you don't have a doctor, there are many websites that can help you calculate what your healthy weight is, based on your height.

Knowing what your goal is will help you plan on how to reach it. It may take a while, but as long as you get there, and stay there when you do, then you have accomplished something very important.

If there is one thing you should take from this book, it's that you really need to treat yourself and your body well. You should know that the main concern of obesity is health, NOT appearance. The health risks associated with obesity are actually deadly. In all seriousness, if you are obese or even overweight, you are at an increased risk for premature death, heart disease, diabetes, and even some types of cancer. No kidding. I've been working in cardiovascular research for years now and trust me, it's a lot easier to prevent disease than to treat it. It's never too late to start treating your body well.

There are many reasons why people gain weight, and most of the time it has nothing to do with being hungry. We often eat to be social or maybe even to gain acceptance. Think of all the gatherings you take part in and how often they happen around a table filled with food. Sometimes, maybe you just want to be polite, so you eat what has been lovingly prepared for you (especially if you have an Italian mother like I do).

More importantly, if you are overweight or obese, it's absolutely vital for you to identify the motives and habits you've developed and replace them with better choices. As mentioned earlier in the book, it could very well be that you are an emotional eater, whether you are feeling sad, guilty or stressed out. However, it's also possible that your eating habits are a symptom of much more serious issues. For that reason, it becomes so very important for you to realize why, when and how you gained the weight in the first place. Be honest with yourself, and do get the help and support you need to face those issues. It may take you a while to make this decision, but in time, I hope you will realize that you can do it, and you are absolutely worth it.

Good luck, be smart and enjoy your fabulous shoes.

Useful

References

There are many websites out there that offer a lot of free and very useful information. I've listed just a few where you can find some really great tips to help you out with meal planning, food shopping and even dining out.

1) www.healthyeating.net

2) www.myamericanheart.org

3) www.nhlbi.nih.gov

4) www.fitness.gov

5) www.healthstatus.com

6) health.yahoo.com

Don't limit yourself. There are many more sites out there that can offer you additional support, including online food diaries and even diet support groups. Don't be afraid to explore on your own to find the help you need.

Bibliography

Esch, T., and G.B. Stefano. 2004. The Neurobiology of Pleasure, Reward Processes, Addiction and their Health Implications. *Neuroendocrinology Letters*. 25 (4): 235-251.

O'Keeffe, L. *Shoes. A Celebration of Pumps, Sandals, Slippers & More.* New York: Workman Publishing Company, Inc., 1996.

Small, D.M., R.J. Zatorre, A. Dagher, A.C. Evans, and M. Jones-Gotman. 2001. Changes in Brain Activity Related to Eating Chocolate: From Pleasure to Aversion. *Brain*. 124: 1720-33.

Wise, R.A. 2002. Brain Reward Circuitry: Insights from Unsensed Incentives. *Neuron*. 36: 229-240.

Food Journal

Date		September, 18, 2006				
Time	Food	Amount	Location	Calories	Mood	Shoe Rating
7:00 AM	Coffee 1% Milk Sugar	2 cups 1/4 cups 1 tsp	Home	8 25 16	Tired	👠👠👠👠👠
8:00 AM	Plain bagel Cream cheese	1 1 tbsp	On the way to work	170 90	Tired	👠👠👠
8:30 AM	Caramel macchiato	16 ounces	At work, before a presentation	250	Stressed	👠👠
12:00 PM	Ham with cheese on bread mayonnaise	4 ounces 4 ounces 4 ounces 1 tb	Lunch in the cafeteria	800	None in particular	👠👠👠
12:00 PM	Water	16 ounces	Lunch in the cafeteria	0	None in particular	👠👠

						TOTAL CALORIES:

Date _____							
Time	Food	Amount	Location	Calories	Mood	Shoe Rating	

						TOTAL CALORIES:

Date	Time	Food	Amount	Location	Calories	Mood	Shoe Rating

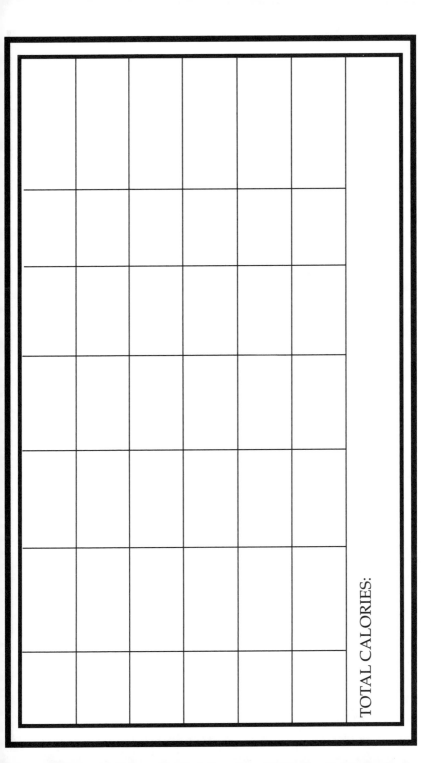

TOTAL CALORIES:

About the author

$\mathcal{D}$r. Isabelle Raymond Shaw is French Canadian, born and raised in Quebec. With a father from the south of France and Italian American mother, her unique heritage makes her appreciate the great diversity of life, namely great food, great fashion and of course, fabulous shoes.

Isabelle has an undergraduate degree in Psychology and obtained both her master's and Ph.D. in Biomedical Science from the University of Montreal . She has always rebelled against the stereotypical scientist "look" and is therefore known to her friends as "the fashion scientist." She currently works in cardiovascular research and resides in St. Louis with her husband and all her shoes.